#POEMS 2

JUDGE THE POET

FOR

CME, SOR AND ADR.

CONTENTS

#POEMS 2

JUDGE THE POET

A FURTHER COLLECTION
OF SHORT POEMS

#Courage

Bright light fears
Are devils
Against destiny.

Twinkling dreams
Are angels
Who set you free.

#Human Rights

Presuming you're human,
And that right isn't wrong,
Shouldn't all human rights
Be our passionate song?

#Muesli

I usually have muesli
And just whistle
As wind breaks in bed.

Then you rudely refused me
So as dawn breaks
It's cornflakes instead.

#Convention

War is war.

We kill theirs,
They kill ours.

The only difference is
We condemn them
For killing ours.

Madness is madness.

#Snowflake

Lazy, dreamy, down they float,
Each picture perfect snowflake.
Giving the world a sugar coat,
Glitter icing on life's cake.

#Wary

Wary of the fact
Reality
Has
Many dimensions

We hold on tight
To the one
Of
Our own invention.

Like birds
In self-made cages.

#Priorities

Prioritise everything
Pleasure as much as work
Friends as much as colleagues
Love as much as success

The soul
Has no
Cash register

#Beware (A Story)

The water beckoned.
He was tempted
By the shadows beneath.

He hadn't reckoned
On the sharpness
Of that shark's teeth.

#Be A Poet

Open windows of belief.
Blow the embers,
Fan the fire.

Paint pictures with your mind.
Dream, dream more
And then inspire.

#Children

Woken by the sound
Of my children's laughter;
Piano butterflies
Circling through sunlit sky.

#Moving

If you're loving,
Keep it moving.
A peaceful pool,
So clear and cool,
Under sun of gold
Can still grow mould.

#Sunday

Late. Early.
Remembrance. Hope.
End. Beginning.

#Glasses

Once we raised
Our glasses
When life matched
Our heart's description.

Now we raise
Our glasses
Which come with
A strong prescription.

#View

This way. That way.
Don't. Go. Stop.
Other side up.

You can't cross here.

Too many signs
Blocking sight lines
In our lives.

#Progress

Shall we make concrete nests,
Fill them with false hopes
And foul the ground
Around us?

We are masters of the world.

#Tears And Years

Tears are liquid,
Yet they burn.
Smiles, though free,
We must earn.
Love is everywhere,
Yet we yearn.
Life is mystery,
We must learn.

#Equality

For as long as we teach

One gender
To care
And one gender
To compete

The sins
Of history
Will simply
Repeat.

#Music

Music and memories
Can live together,
Forever,
Hand in glove.

Floating and fluttering,
Stirring, recurring,
Recalling
Souls in love.

#Ant

An ant atop
His forest throne
Surveys the kingdom
As proudly as
The mightiest beast.

#Book Of Life

Life turns each page,
Youth turns to age.

Forgotten chapters
For every season
Find no sense or end.
Feelings are reason.

HAIKUS

#Silence
Sweet songs, forgotten.
When they were very last sung,
Did anyone cry?

#Foreign Policy
More money misused.
Murky, murderous moments.
Madness and mayhem.

#Love
Love is compassion.
Love, without belief, is myth.
Compassion is love.

#Human
The human spirit.
Remarkable creation.
It's unbrea
kable.

#Wake Up

Morning sky
Painted colours divine
With defiant beauty
Of shade and line.
Beauty revealed
To be adored,
So often accepted
Or ignored.

#First Step

The first step...
To getting better:
Saying "I am ill."
To finding out:
Saying "I don't know."
To achieving:
Having a dream.

#Election

Political mendacity,
Electoral fun and frolics.
Some call it disingenuous,
I just call it bo****ks.

#Time Out

Children play
As adults fight.
Inventively.
Endlessly.
Sometimes cruel,
Always fervent,

When will
The game end?

#Caveman (A Story)

And his whole
Face smiled
At his hole.

Deep delight
For the
Troglodite.

Easier love
Than that
Up above.

#Trust

Trust is oxygen
In the bloodstream
Of real love
And friendship's dream.

Trust abused.
Body aching.
Deep and far
Beyond heartbreaking.

#Poem

The cat sat
On the mat.
Fact.

The black cat
Sat on the
Rough mat.
Story.

Why did the
Black cat
Sit on the
Rough mat?
Poem.

#Fortune

What difference a letter makes.
A great divider can be wealth;
A great leveller can be health.
Fortune gives and fortune takes.

#War

The honest lives
Of children,
Husbands, wives...

'Til warring breath
Blows the stench
Of death.

Peace.
In pieces.

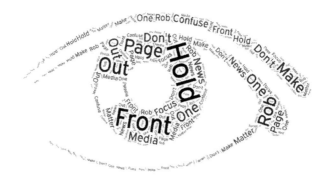

#Hold The Front Page

Out of 100,000
One may rob you.
But 99,999
Don't make the news.

No matter what is
All about you,
That media focus
Can often confuse.

#Foolish

Foolishly,
Children believe
Adults
Are settled and sure.

Some foolish
Adults believe
Children
Have smaller spirits.

#Advertising

Creative advertising
Can make the ordinary
Look quite surprising.

The emperor's new clothes
Artfully hung to dry
On Pinocchio's nose.

#Civilisation

Rule Number One:
No Rules.

Then fools
Made Rule
Number Two...

And overruled
Number One
By committee
And by gun.

#Call

Call.
Carpet.
Of honour.
Bread.
Wallpaper.
Rock and.
Toilet tissue.
Don't stop me.
I'm on a roll.

#Seize Life

With every pound of joy,
An ounce of regret.
As the sun starts to rise,
We know it must set.

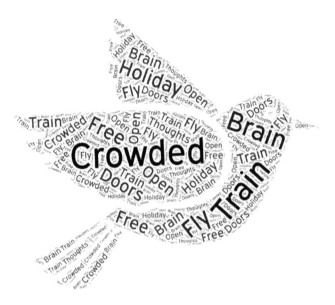

#Holiday

A
Crowded brain
Is
Like a
Crowded train.

Doors open.

Thoughts
Fly free.

#Menu

True and fiery love
Is fresh, spicy food,
Making life full and rich.

Calculating love
Is like digesting
A plastic-wrapped sandwich.

#Is This You?

You used to want
To save or change
The world.

Now you just want
To save or change
Your mortgage.

#Life Cycle

When it's flowing,
Keep it going.

Fall off, feel pain,
Get on again.

If facts deceive,
You must believe.

Ride on.

#The Future

I won't copy
Those mistakes.

I won't repeat
Those lies.

My hopes
Will remain high.

HAIKUS

#Art
Art has no rules, so
Learn all the rules of art
And then break them.

#Possibly
Impossible dreams.
Love. Peace. Unity. Respect.
Impossible dreams?

#Vision
I see the mirror.
An old man looks back at me,
Waiting quietly.

#Luck
There is only luck.
Not good luck or bad. Just luck.
See it. Feel it. Live.

#Spring

Bright
Light

Frosts
Clear
Shoots
Appear

Winter
Splinters

Fresh
Young
Spring
Sprung

New hope

#All Sorts

Big people, small people,
All shapes and sizes.
One of life's great joys...
Corporeal surprises.

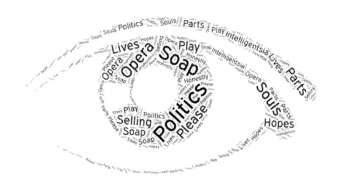

#Politics

Politics:
Soap opera
For the Intelligentsia,
Selling not soap
But lives, hopes
And souls.

So please
Play your parts
Honestly.

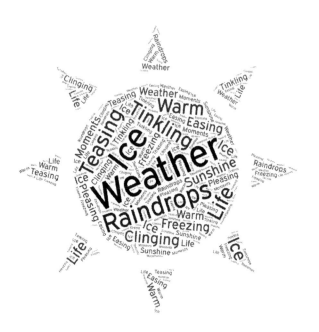

#Weather

Tinkling raindrops, teasing.
Clinging ice, freezing.
Warm sunshine, easing.
Life's moments, pleasing.

#Blank

Blank minds
And
Blank hearts
Are

Blank accounts
Which earn
No interest.

#Old

Secret lies, miniature histories,
Tearful eyes, unsolved mysteries,
Touching loves, fables untold...
The mental matrix of being old.

#Poetry

Poetry is so
Low-tech.

It can only
Engage
Your imagination,
Your mind, your heart.

And move your soul.

No wonder it's so cheap.

#Riches

See the crying baby
Perfectly
Born.

Witness the criminal
Casually
Yawn.

And choose your way.

#Unmoney

Not stacks of toy tokens,
Inheritance,
Privilege unspoken...

But credits for kindness,
Effort and care,
Accepted everywhere.

#Joy (A Story)

Blinded by joy.

My dreams
Were crushed
Beneath
Her starlit wings.

Sometimes
Beauty
Is the beast.

#Riddle

A riddle's satisfaction:
Word and thought interaction.
A pleasing, heady potion;
Like poetry in motion.

#Then And Now

When I thought
I was
Preparing
For my life,

I did not
Realise
That was part
Of my life.

#Magic

Words are keys to
Unlock musical thoughts
And feelings.

Thoughts and feelings
Unlock your mind, soul
And future.

114

#Motto

If it's slow,
If it's quick,
If it's short,
If it's long.

It doesn't matter.

As long
As it's true.

#Peace

Fighting
For peace
Is like
Boiling a kettle
For cold water.

You might get there.

But it's
A long,
Expensive,
Stupid
Way to do it.

#Value

I'm not the richest
Or the poorest.
Like most people
It seems.

Privilege, justice
Are not with me.
But they can't take
My dreams.

#A Critic

Finding clever things to say
Is no way to spend a day.
And I don't want to sound snobbish
But some of your rhymes are
rubbish.

#Forever

We bring out
The best
And the worst
In each other.

Expecting
The best,
We criticise
The worst.

This is True Love.

#Dream

Dream,
And the world dreams
With you.

Despair,
And it all
Goes wrong.

Solo
Grumbling is
Not new.

United,
We are brave
And strong.

#Puzzle

The universe:
A jigsaw puzzle
Shattered into
Infinite pieces.

Our mission:
To polish and colour
The pieces and
Reassemble.

HAIKUS

#Is This You?
Do broken mirrors
Of youthful ideals reflect
Your reality?

#My Words
My words aren't opaque,
Neither are they transparent.
They are translucent.

#Scars
Scars and blemishes
We pick up along the way
Make us who we are.

#Notice
We have everything.
So much. And yet we notice
Virtually nothing.

#Embrace

So excited
By things that
Are not real,

We forget
To embrace,
Taste and feel

The actual deal.

#Survivor

Hi
story…
My
Story:
My
stery,
Mi
sery.

A
Life.
A
live.
Sure
I've
Sur
vived.

You must too.

#Science

I know I am an Artist,
So my theory won't impress.
But, let's face it, most Science
Is simply the last best guess.

#True

True love
Has no
Conditions

Only
Hopeful
Certainty.

#Places

Do places
Have souls?

A nest:
To nurture,
To rest,
Progress.

A cauldron:
To curse,
To crush,
To choke.

Environment
Or destiny?

#For Edward Lear

Can you wave across the ocean?
Can you reign across the sky?
Can you make a cat a pillar?
Can you make some butter fly?

#Another Day

Nightmares of
Insignificance
Punish
The faint-hearted.

There is only
One way:
Forwards.

#Rulers

Your mansion shares a street
With homes
The size of tissue boxes.

These are issue boxes
When hopes
Are the size of our homes.

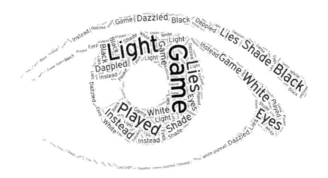

#The Game

The game is played:
Not black, white.
Not light or shade.

Instead our eyes
Are dazzled
With dappled lies.

#Work

Their works
Became noticed,
Appreciated
And considered
Important,
Only after
Their death.

Say it quickly.
It doesn't
Hurt,
So much.

#If Music Be The Food Of Love

The unspoken
Can shout
To the undeaf ear.

Love is obvious
To those
You truly hold dear.

#Out

Like dew
On the grass
In the morning

Or sweat
On a brow
Without warning

Hypocrisy
Will reveal
Itself.

#Coffee

Strange, bitter,
Yet it brings
Delight.

Deep darkness
Which makes us
See bright.

#Morality

Is it simply
Expedient
To ignore each
Ingredient

In order to
Savour
The lusted for
Flavour?

#Truth

You have to separate
What inspires
Something
From what that
Something
Actually means.

Otherwise
You're an idiot.

#Young And Old

Young people are fireworks:
Fresh, inspired.
Old people are streetlights:
So admired.
Middle-aged people are
Being rewired.

#Think About It

I met my Destiny
And blew it.
That was my Destiny,
I knew it.

#Position

Don't be too breezy
Or make it easy

For those you
Disagree with
To hold sway.

They also serve
Who only stand
In the way.

#Be

Exist.
Persist.

Resist
The fog
Of false thought

Which turns
All being
Into sport.

#Together

Striving towards a worthy goal,
Each single act affects the whole.
Let's work together without schism:
It's Collective Individualism.

HAIKUS

#Gone
Vanished without trace,
Explosions across her face.
Not smiles, nor wrinkles.

#Time
It's hard, in winter,
To recall a summer's warmth.
Old age forgets youth.

#One
Each one that makes it
Hides one thousand who do not.
Some worse, some better.

#Feel
Have we been misled?
Not power or position...
To feel is to live.

#Circle Of Life

The circle of life
Never ends
Or begins

It just
Spins
And
Spins

The circle of life
Never ends
Or begins

It just
Spins
And...

#Shake

Shake free
Your chains,
See what
Remains.

Are you defined
By your chains?

#Reality

Shakespeare wrote to his mum,
Fonteyn walked across the floor,
Mozart whistled in the bath,
Da Vinci painted his back door.

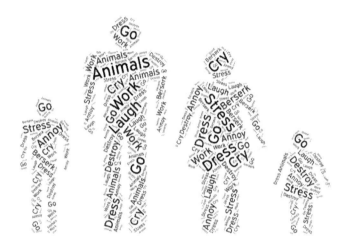

#Animals

We dress,
We stress,
We go to work.

The animals laugh at us.

We annoy,
We destroy,
We go berserk.

The animals cry for us.

#Reflect

Don't expect me to be perfect,
The cost isn't worth the price.
I am who I am who I am...
Not simple or faultless, just nice.

#Pitch

Life's a campsite.

Some coming,
Some going.
Some setting up,
Some taking down.

A collective
Of individuals
Who share
Or ignore.

#Media

Can't we be simply informed
No pyrotechnics performed?
Some media sweat and grovel,
And show life like a cheap novel.

#Tradition (A Story)

The fog of tradition
Obscured
The pinnacles of possibility.
Until,
One day,
The sunshine of promise
Blazed.

#Rush

Seeing paths we have chosen,
Knowing where they have led,
I feel gratitude and blessing...
A rush of love to the head.

#Hope

Hope is
Belief
Without
The signposts.

#Poet's Mantra

Who needs verse?
Well universe,
You need verse!

#One Flame In A Fire

Sense of Self
Is an
Illusion.

We are all
The same
Mass of Magic

Poured into
Different-shaped pots.

#I Don't Get What You Don't Get

Peace.
Love.
Protect the Planet.

I don't get
What you don't get.

#Fear

As night-time mist
Clouds
The brightness of day,

So hopeless doubt
Shrouds
Hearts made to play.

#Writing

This is not reality.
This is just a bookshelf.
I offer words and ask
That you think for yourself.

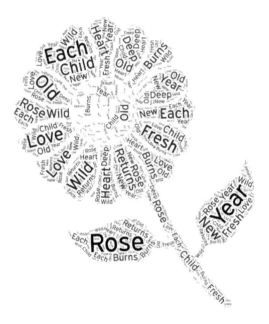

#Rose

Each year
The rose returns
Fresh as a child.

Each year
My heart burns
Deep and wild.

Love is old,
Love is new.

#Meaning Of Life

Do no harm,
Help if you can.
Collect experiences,
Which are feelings.

Simple.

#Destination

You may
Shout loud
And be wrong.

We will
Stay calm
And be right.

If your act is hate,
Our reply will be love.

Our peace
Will be
Your end.

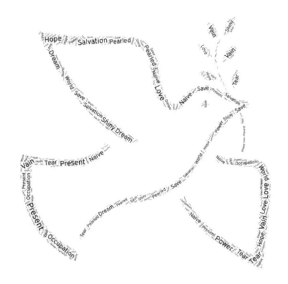

#Present

It's not a naïve
Or vain occupation
To love, hope
And dream of salvation

Every tear
Shiny and pearled
Has a power
To save the world

#Future

Back to villages.
And beyond. Our destiny.
Return to nature.

JUDGE THE POET

ABOUT THE AUTHOR

JUDGE THE POET has been creating and performing poems all around the globe, for every kind of audience, for nearly three decades.

His humble aim is to change the world of/through poetry.

JUDGE lives in England with his partner and their two children.

Printed in Great Britain
by Amazon